Holy IT!

The Amazing Power of ClarITy

Rick,
I Hope You
Enjoy IT!
— Scott

A Guide to Finding and Doing Your Thing – Your 'IT'

SCOTT WITTIG

Holy IT!
Written by Scott Wittig
Design by Debra Davis Rezeli
Illustration by Jim Nuttle

2009 Published by Achieve IT Media. All rights reserved.

Scott Wittig
[scott@scottwittig.com]
www.holyitbook.com

ISBN 1449918360
EAN-13 9781449918361

SECOND PRINTING

Printed in the U.S.

For Jeanne and my kids, Ella & Kyle.
Thanks for letting me go upstairs so much.

Contents

Introduction

What are you doing about what you aren't doing?

Huh?

It is a heck of a question and helping you answer it is the driving force of this book. Many of us have our antennae up for the things that are important to us at any given time. It might be that you have been eyeballing a Mini Cooper to put in your driveway, so now everywhere you look there is a Mini Cooper. You may be working on a project at work that involves helping your company to be environmentally friendly, so now every newspaper article and story on the news about "going green" grabs your interest. You have a new baby on the way, so now you notice styles of strollers.

My antennae are up when I hear people say things like:

I wish I could ...

If I didn't have to work I would ...

Someday I'm going to ...

... but I can't do that now because ...

When I get around to it I will ...

Everyone has something that they either want to be doing or absolutely should be doing based on their strengths, interests, talents and abilities. I once posed this question to a life and business coach who has coached hundreds of people – "How many people that you coach are actually serving out their purpose at work?" His estimation was less than

50%. That means that half of us are not doing what we should be doing to serve our purpose for being on this earth; our talents and strengths may be utilized in our daily work, but they aren't being utilized in the most impactful way possible. What a waste!

"Death isn't the greatest loss in life. The greatest loss is what dies inside of us while we live." — Norman Cousins

Try it – the next time you are on a trip with your family, on the phone with a friend or talking to a business colleague, step out and ask the question – "Everybody has something they *aren't* doing that they wish they *were* doing – what's yours?" You will almost always get an answer that is either outside of what they do in their work life or something they are blowing off at work that they should totally be doing! The answers will range from "writing a book" to "following through on an idea that I have for a really cool product" to "creating a business plan instead of flying by the seat of my pants everyday" – and everywhere in-between. What you hear may floor you because it may expose a part of the person that you never knew...

and that is where the magic is – in their heart.

The heart of the person is where this answer lies and that is where the passion for this thing – their "IT" as I will describe later – is lying in wait.

"There are many things that will catch my eye, but there are only a few that catch my heart. It is those I consider to pursue." — Tim Redmond

This book is designed to take that (sometimes uncomfortable) question that helps determine "IT" and go one step further by asking "What are you willing to do about it?" If the answer is "nothing," then this book is not for you. If the answer is "I don't know, but I'm darn sure going to find out," then read on.

IN ACTION
INACTION

Do you see the difference?

There is a space, literally pressing the space bar on the keyboard, between the words "in action" and "inaction." That's it - a space. But the difference is huge. It probably takes the same amount of time to hit the space bar as it does for your mind to go to the wired-default that too many of us suffer from – "Don't do it, it'll be too hard, just keep doing what you're doing." It's during that space in time that we have to be able to stop and remind ourselves just how important our cause, our muse, our purpose – **our IT** – really is.

Flick the devil of inaction off your shoulder to make room for the angel that is action.

Action is what this book is about. As odd is it may sound, my hope is to *inspire* hope. My wish is that you will go through this book, be an active participant with an open mind and that you will return to it as a reference on a regular basis. This is not a *read it and leave it* book. It's much more important that you read it with the belief that you *can* change. Seth Godin says, "Quit or be exceptional. Average is for losers." Pretty bold, but his point is well-taken.

For you to go all-in when it comes to taking action on a task, you must believe that what you are doing is tied to something bigger. *Something bigger* may be related to spirituality or religion, or not. It may be about a cause, a company or a movement. The steps and exercises within these pages will help you determine what the bigger thing is. No matter what IT is, IT is important and IT need not lie dormant anymore.

Being that we are all very different, I want to go ahead and get one of my quirky traits out on the table. I have the ability to put really whacky, unrelated things together into thoughts and ideas. "Disparate facts into related uses" is the fancy way to put that. An example is that I own a piece of land that has no house on it. I got caught up in the real estate boom and buying it "sounded like a good idea at the time." There is no way that I am aware of to generate revenue from a plot of dirt while you are trying to sell it, but if I could get Google to pay me to spray paint "GOOGLE WAS HERE" on it, take a picture of it from space and put it on Google Earth just as a funny thing to do, that might get me a little money to offset the payment or even pay it off! Yeah, that's the kind of "disparate information" that my mind will link together into "related uses."

With that said, I am going to take you back to your teenage years when you went through Driver Education and use lessons learned from it to guide you through this book. Of course - Driver Ed and taking action on your IT - makes total sense! It will, I promise.

In Driver Ed they often use the acronym IPDE. It stands for Identify – Predict – Determine – Execute. It isn't a sexy, memorable acronym, but it is a very effective way to learn how to drive. First you have to

Identify that there is something in the road, then you have to

Predict what that "thing" in the road is going to do (or do to your car if you hit it), then you have to

Determine what you are going to do and then you must

Execute on that decision.

It is a great thought process to learn and make habitual. Hang on to this analogy as we use IPDE to help you Identify, Predict, Determine and Execute your IT.

You are going to see these two words in various places throughout the book. There is huge value in finding silence and solitude; not only to lower your stress level, decompress and let go of the day, but to let your natural inclinations and the answers to some tough questions rise to the surface. I believe that we can help ourselves figure out an awful lot if given the time to be quiet.

Daniel Harkavy, owner of Building Champions, trains his life & business coaches to strive for a 70/30 ratio with their time – let their clients talk 70% of the time and the coaches speak only 30% of the time. Put another way, allow people to figure things out on their own as much as possible. When you are able to do this it allows you to own IT – your thought or idea, or your purpose - passion - project as we will discuss later.

So, when you see [**GET QUIET**], make an effort to actually do so. Take a few minutes to re-read a section of the book or to reflect on some of the thoughts and feelings that arose as you read the words on the page.

"If you want good results, you need to perform good actions. If you want to perform good actions, you must have positive expectations. To have positive expectations, you have to first believe." – John Maxwell

IT

We start with *IT* rather than *DO* because you can't *DO* it
until you know what *IT* is that you want to *DO*!

*There comes a special moment in everyone's life, a moment for which
that person was born. That special opportunity, when he seizes it, will
fulfill his mission—a mission for which he is uniquely qualified. In that
moment, he finds greatness. It is his finest hour.*

— Winston Churchill

Identify

He slept beneath the moon; He basked beneath the sun;
He lived a life of going-to-do; And died with nothing done.
— English playwright James Albery

In hindsight, reading that quote was probably the impetus for starting my groups and writing this book, even though I first read it years ago. I am an idea guy. I am constantly coming up with ideas for products, inventions, websites - you name it. If ever I have a title within my own entity it will probably be "Chief Idea Guy." Taking every idea all the way to fruition on my own? Um, not so much. But when I read that quote, I realized that it doesn't take too long to lose credibility when you share ideas with others and don't act on them. So I set out to figure out how to become a doer. How do you shift from being a talker to a doer? You uncover or identify your purpose, your passion, or your project - your IT.

"..nothing will lower your self-esteem
more rapidly than breaking agreements."
—Sally McGhee

I determined a few years back that I wanted to positively impact as many lives as possible and do so in a big way. Over time, and through the help of coaching, I figured out my true purpose in life. I have boiled it down to three words:

HELP OTHERS ACHIEVE.

Before I started being coached, I had no idea what purpose was all about – I had never really thought about it. I had gone through my work and personal lives with no guiding force, none that I was conscious of at least. Then I went through a series of exercises and did a bunch of reading. I can tell you that figuring IT out is a game-changer.

I had come up with all of these ideas and inventions and done nothing. Why? Because I hadn't tied them to something bigger. However, with the idea for this book and for my groups, I pulled it all together and *I KEPT COMING BACK TO IT.* That's how you know you've got IT....you've figured IT out.....when you come back to IT over and over and over.

You think of something that you may want to do or an idea for a business
and then life gets busy.

You go to a conference and walk out with a mile-long list of ideas to improve your business & change the world
and then life gets busy.

You start to work on a new initiative that you really believe in at work
and then life gets busy.

How do you know what's important, what you should be doing? *YOU COME BACK TO IT.* You feel like something is missing. Your juices get flowing every time you talk about it. You lay down at night and everything gets quiet and you can't go to sleep because you can't stop thinking about it. You've found your IT!

"Nothing is more dangerous than an idea when it is the only one you have." – Emile Chartier

Once you figure IT out,

...you will feel like you just made friends with the biggest kid in class...on the first day of school. — John Eldredge

CHAPTER 1
The 3 P's - Purpose, Passion or Project?

I struggled as I began working on the outline for this book. Trying to figure out who you, my reader, was going to be was very difficult. As I said earlier, one of my big, hairy, audacious goals (BHAGs) is to affect as many lives as possible in a positive way. Figuring out the messaging that was needed and the audience I wanted to reach in order to accomplish this BHAG led to a thought process that went something like this –

Who do I speak to? Who are my people? Am I going to affect the most lives by speaking about life purpose and trying to get people to start working inside of their purpose on a daily basis?

Dude, it's been done already by people a lot smarter than you. Heck, Oprah's on the case.

Don't reinvent the wheel.

Plus, maybe talking about purpose and suggesting ways to "be purposeful" will be lost on a lot of people.

So, maybe it's passion we should work on.

Yeah, that's it - maybe people will "get it" if I talk about passion and what their muse is….

...then it hit me that there is a crucial distinction to be made when trying to determine your IT. I call them the 3 P's –

Purpose

Passion

Project

You, as the reader, may be one of the lucky ones who has identified your purpose
.... or not.

You may already be working on your passion on a regular basis
.... or not.

You may be working on the projects that you need to in order to reach fulfillment of your vision
.... or not.

Regardless of where you are on your determination journey and where you fit in terms of having figured out the 3 P's, committing some time to reflect on them will prove to be invaluable.

It does not take much strength to do things, but it requires a great deal of strength to decide what to do. – Elbert Hubbard

So much light could be shed on our lives if we would explore what we were meant to be before things (went another way). What were we created to do? – John Eldredge

Purpose | Def. - The action for which a person or thing is specially fitted or used, or for which a thing exists.

Identifying the purpose of your life is one of the most raw, fundamental and powerful exercises that you can perform. Whether you believe that it is God's doing or simply a truth – you *are* here for a reason. How depressing might it be to go through life without believing that in some form or fashion?

There have been some phenomenal books written about purpose, such as Rick Warren's, *The Purpose Driven Life* and *A New Earth by Eckart Tolle*. Oprah Winfrey created an entire online classroom around Tolle's work. All of this has brought a great deal of attention to the power of identifying your purpose. Identifying your purpose is a journey; a journey that can have a lot of twists and turns that you may never expect. I encourage you to utilize these books and tools as well as the exercises at the end of this section to help you down that road.

I had never understood the importance of being "on purpose" until I hired a coach. Starting in 2003, I went through a year-long process that, among other things, helped me to create an envisioned future; my vision. The major component of this vision document was to identify, and connect with, my purpose. As a Mortgage Loan Officer I wrote,

To give honest financial advice to clients in order to positively contribute to their financial well-being.

That was my purpose in life, to give honest financial advice? Nope, that wasn't it but I went with it. Remember when I said this is a journey? It worked for me at the time, so the frame I used when writing out my vision was around that statement.

Fast-forward three years to another round of coaching with the same company, but a different coach. I went through the exact same process in terms of the order and structure of the coaching sessions and used most of the same tools. However, this time we stopped on the unbelievably important area of identifying purpose *for what seemed like an eternity!* We worked on it, worked on it and worked on it. Jamey, my coach, made me read a book called *Waking the Dead* by John Eldredge. What I learned was that your purpose is your purpose is your purpose. It is not dependent on anything external – the task does not determine the purpose. I had been framing my purpose around whichever account of my life I was thinking about at the time. I had hired a coach for help with my business, so I framed the process of identifying my purpose around work. *To give honest financial advice to clients in order to positively contribute to their financial well-being.* But that is not why I was put here. What about my family? What about some other business I may create? What about volunteer work that I might do?

With the help of that book and my coach's brilliant insight, it became abundantly clear that your purpose is not dependent on anything else. It is the thing for which you are specially fitted. It can be applied to virtually everything you do. So, after much tweaking and many fits and starts, my purpose surfaced and it is summarized in three words that you read earlier,

HELP OTHERS ACHIEVE.

Those three words were, for all intents and purposes, in the original purpose statement – *To give honest financial advice to clients in order to positively contribute to their financial well-being* – but all of the other words around them clouded those three words and kept them from standing out.

I equate this process to a walk on the beach. Have you ever been on the beach walking against a heavy wind? It can be very difficult. You feel a little bit overwhelmed. All the resistance, noise and sensation makes you question what you are doing out there.

Then you turn around and it's a whole new experience.

You now have the wind at your back. You feel supported and more confident. Your head is up instead of down. This is how I felt once I got those three words out of my heart, onto paper and then out of my mouth to someone else. I'll tell you, if it all feels a little "wispy," remind yourself that a little humility can take you a long way.

[GET QUIET]

Notes:

Do what you love, and the pleasure
of doing what you love will follow.

– You, Inc.

Passion | Def. - A strong wish for something

Have you ever had a Jerry McGuire moment? One part of that movie has Tom Cruise working feverishly through the night on a document that he believed would change his industry for the better. He gets multiple copies made for everyone in his firm, hands them out, makes a speech - and then gets fired for it. However, he believed so strongly in his idea that he went out on his own - on a budget, driven by his passion - and ultimately had success.

Your moment may have gone like this if you had one like Jerry's - your head hit the pillow just like every other night, everything got quiet and BOOM, it hit you. You got up, went to the computer and wrote out your speech or sketched the layout for the website you could sell to Yahoo! for $600M or drew a mockup for plastic clogs with holes in them that every kid would just have to have.

What do you have once that moment has passed and you've spit out the initial idea? You have *passion* - for the idea, for what it can do for others, for the possibilities. You likely fall into one of three areas when it comes to passion:

1. You've had your defining moment like Jerry and have identified your passion.

2. You have a passion that has always been with you.

3. You are reading this book in hopes that you will come out on the other side with your passion identified.

No matter which category you are in, it is likely that your passion stems from something you are already good at, something you have familiarity with.

You may have taken a photography class in college
*....and you have a **passion** for taking pictures.*

You may have been a tremendous athlete in high school
*....and you have a **passion** for Friday night football.*

You may have always had dogs throughout your life
*....and you have a **passion** for keeping animals safe.*

The beautiful things about passion are that it is steady, it is well-founded and it is likely based on talent. Socrates said, "To move the world we must first move ourselves." This thing - your IT - is something that has already moved you in some way. As you identify it, you will then be able to use it to move others.

I had my Jerry McGuire moment in 2006. My head was on the pillow. The lights were off. It was quiet – everywhere except in my head. So, at about one in the morning, I went to my computer and wrote a speech. I didn't just punch the keys, I immediately knew *when* and *where* I was going to give that speech. More importantly, I knew *why* – I was going to move people and move them to action. Here is an excerpt from the original speech:

(Powerpoint slide up on the screen behind me says ACTS ☺)

I know you're wondering what ACTS ☺ means. "*Acts* happy" doesn't describe me, but it used to. Here's how the story goes – guy comes up with idea, guy writes letter and sends it to best-selling author and renowned speaker, Todd Duncan and sends another copy to Daniel Harkavy, owner of wildly-successful coaching company, Building Champions. In said letter, guy explains idea, asks for their help with it and then proceeds to tell them that he tried to kill himself twice when he was in high school.

HUH?

Yeah, I thought it was crazy to send that letter too......but I did it! I went through a time in my life where I acted happy. I wasn't at all, but I acted that way. In actuality, I felt like there was a black cloud hanging over my head that was never going to go away, so I tried to off myself twice.....then I decided to find something that I was actually good at!

(laughter – I hope)

I call that "finding my **IT**." What was **IT**? For me, **IT** was developing a sincere interest in others and helping them. **IT** was listening more than I talked. **IT** was sharing knowledge and experiences that would help them out. **IT** was doing anything that I could to keep people from being too hard on themselves.

Todd Duncan is like a rock star in the mortgage industry. Every industry has "that guy" who everyone looks up to, buys products and services from and who everyone respects. I sent a letter and a copy of my speech to him because *I was sure* I was going to give that speech *at his event!* I copied Daniel Harkavy on the letter because I was going to get him to *give up some of his speaking time to me at Todd's event* because *I was sure that Daniel and I were going to work on this project together.* I didn't know these guys and quite honestly, they were the type of guys who made my palms sweaty if I got anywhere near the opportunity to talk to them.

Can you guess what the first word was that came out of Daniel's mouth when I called him to see what he thought about my speech? *Passion.* Your passion is in you and hopefully it is rising to the surface as you read this.

[GET QUIET]

Notes:

You can't DO purpose.
You can't DO passion.
But, you can DO projects.

Project | Def. - A planned undertaking

For the majority of us, there is something in our way; something that we know we should be doing but we aren't. Elmer Letterman said, "The average human being in any line of work could double his productive capacity overnight if he began right now to do all the things he knows he should do, and stop doing all the things he knows he should not do." What's yours?

Is it going out on your own?

Are you a Realtor who wants the whole commission instead of splitting it with your broker? Are you a web designer who is tired of working inside of someone else's creative guidelines? Are you a CPA for a major corporation who knows that you can make more money with less stress?

Is it something as simple as writing a business plan...and sticking to it?

Do you write one every year and then throw it in the drawer? Are you oblivious when it comes to determining what to do next because you don't have a plan? Are you a "yes man" because you have nothing guiding your daily actions?

Is it losing weight or getting back into shape?

Are you a workaholic who "has no time" to exercise? Have you joined a gym or started a diet and then let that practice wane away before it could become a habit? Are you experiencing chest pain just reading this book?

Heck, the answer to the last question may be the answer to all of them! Stress comes from not knowing what to do next. Stress comes from not knowing what the outcome of an action might be. Stress comes from indecision. Stress comes from an inability or unwillingness to take action.

I've been a stress-ball over the last few years. I have had so many ideas for businesses, books, websites, coaching others, etc. (write to me and I'll send you the list). The idea that has consumed me most has been around the creation of *"do IT groups™."* You will read more about these groups in 'The Power of Groups' section at the end of this book, but I will share a bit with you here.

The idea of the mastermind group has been around for a long, long time. It is essentially a knowledge-share where you get together to help others with challenges they are facing in business or in life. I had the epiphany of creating a format for mastermind groups that would blend together the essential herbs and spices for a successful group interaction.

After developing the idea a bit, I called my friend Andy Beal and said, "I've come up with a format for a mastermind group that will help people who have ideas or inventions or challenges that they are not acting on. It will provide them with some guidance on what to do next and offer accountability tools to ensure that they get these things done. Do you know of anyone who would benefit from such a group?" Can you guess what he said?

"Yeah, I know someone – **YOU!**"
Thanks a lot, Andy.
(sarcasm intended)

Andy wrote a book called *Radically Transparent.* The book evangelizes the idea that we need to be more open and honest. We need to admit flaws and mistakes. We need to manage our reputation. So here I am being transparent with you. Yes, the author of the book you hold in your hands – this book about getting things done that you're not doing – has just told you that he needs help on a regular basis to determine the best next action to take and to be held accountable to getting those things done. I am being radically transparent in hopes that it helps you to understand that, as David Allen said, "We're all alone in this together." I have fought my way through the daily challenges of being a husband, father and mortgage guy (through the absolute worst and best two years that the industry has ever experienced) to deliver this book to you, learned how to speak concisely about it and formed *do IT groups* so that I could fulfill on my purpose in life. You can do IT too!

[GET QUIET]

Notes:

✻

You have learned about determining one of your 3 P's in this chapter – your IT. I have framed it this way in hopes of reaching the masses and helping as many people as I can. You may have determined that "picking" one of these 3 P's may be above you, beneath you or at the right level. The major "ah-hah" for some of you may have been the same "ah-hah" that I got when I sat down with Dr. Robert Elliott.

Dr. Elliott has one of the most respected and successful pediatric dental offices in the country. He is Board Certified, a Diplomate with the American Board of Pediatric Dentistry and a Fellow with The American Academy of Pediatric Dentistry. The dude is no joke, and he's a great friend of mine so I can call him *dude*. One night, I had dinner with him to tell him about this book and ask him if I could interview him for it one day. Well, the interview ended up happening right then and there! It was pretty short and went something like this,

> Me – "So I'm writing a book that is going to help people identify their 'thing' or 'IT' that they know they should be doing, but aren't. We all have one, you know."

> Him – (glazed look that says to me that he really doesn't get that this is true)

> Me – "I'm going to help people determine theirs by talking about purpose, passion or project so that I can make sure I reach as many people as I can."

> I went on to explain the differences in the 3 P's and then asked him, "If I was to ask you, which one would you say that you are living out in your practice?"

> Him – "ALL THREE!"

> Me – "Well, there's my *ah-hah* for the end of the first section of the book!"

We could all be so lucky!

Dr. Elliott has truly found his thing for which he is "properly fitted," that he has a "strong wish for" and that leads to many successful "planned undertakings." He has found all of his 3 P's in one vocation. As I've spoken with him over the years, it has become abundantly clear how passionate he is about what he does and how much he believes that he was put here to take care of kids. All of the projects that he has completed – from teaching dental students at the schools that he attended, to planning for and building a state-of-the-art new office, to taking on a partner to ensure that his legacy continues after he is out of the daily practice – have all occurred after a relatively easy decision-making process because he had a filter. His filter is his "something bigger" that you read about earlier – *help as many kids as possible to have healthy smiles and a positive attitude about dental care.*

Would teaching pediatric dental students how to excel in their field *help more kids have healthy smiles and a positive attitude about dental care?*
√ **Decision made** – *spend time as an adjunct professor*

Would building a state-of-the-art new office with flat screens everywhere (including over the chairs so the kids can watch a flick while they are getting their teeth cleaned) *help more kids have healthy smiles and a positive attitude about dental care?*
√ **Decision made** – *build the mack-daddy new office*

Would sacrificing a big percentage of income in the short-term by taking on another Dentist as a partner *help more kids have healthy smiles and a positive attitude about dental care?*
√ **Decision made** – *bring on the second Dentist*

What I want you to see is that these kinds of enormous, potentially taxing and stressful decisions can be made a whole lot easier if you have found your IT. This becomes your filter for deciding whether or not to do something OR what you should be doing, period. All too often, your best intentions are derailed by what *someone else* thinks you should be doing.

In Dr. Elliott's case, he has –

Been invited to speak at national conferences
...and said no.
Been asked to be the President of state organizations
...and said no.
Been asked to serve as an expert witness in court cases
...and said no.

All of these requests of his time have been flattering and could be considered career-enhancing, but he declined the opportunities because they didn't make it through his filter.

What's yours? Do you have a filter? A set of core values, a guiding force, a defined purpose for getting out of bed and doing what you do? What are the requests that are regularly made of your time that you say yes to, but probably shouldn't?

Does your boss tell you to start calling on a company you've never even heard of
...and you say yes because _____

Do friends ask you to go to weekend meetings in hotel ballrooms about "business opportunities"
...and you say yes because _____

Do you get asked to go to lunch by the guy at work who is always talking-down the job
...and you say yes because _____

Once you have determined your IT you will be driving your own car. Instead of just climbing into the backseat and letting everyone around you drive your car throughout the day or throughout your life, you'll be at the helm. You'll be making decisions as to what to do and what not to do. You'll feel like someone has taken a sledgehammer to your stone shoes.

John Eldredge said, "What would happen if you believed it, if you came to the place where you *knew* it was true? Your life would never be the same." My hope is that your life will never be the same after identifying and acting on IT.

"..when one has a passionate sense of purpose, energy rises, obstacles become incidental, and perseverance wins out." – John Maxwell

[GET QUIET]

You will learn later about how incredibly valuable the help of others can be, especially when identifying IT. My hope is that the exercises that follow this section will help you to have the same success that I did with this process. There is a sense of self-exploration in the first set of questions. Following that you will be asked to enlist the help of others to help you determine your IT.

EXERCISE

Ask yourself.....

If money was no matter, what would I do in my work life?

When my feet hit the ground in the morning, what drives me the most?

Who do I believe is best-served by my talents?

What am I capable of that delivers the most value to those around me?

What skill or strength do I have that is or could be most impactful on others?

What values do I hold most dear?

"When I grow up I'm going to be a _____." How did I answer that as a child? What was my original job description?

What is my purpose in life?

Why did God put me here?

What is getting in my way?

[Harder] EXERCISE –
Ask others.....

What should I stop doing?

What can you count on me for?

What can I do better?

What am I best at?

What do you think I should be doing that I'm not doing?

What is my purpose in life?

Who should I stay away from?

Predict

He who deliberates fully before taking a step will spend his entire life on one leg. — Chinese Proverb

There are times in life when we are taken out of our comfort zone. I would count being admitted to the hospital or wearing a cast as two of those moments. I experienced both recently (via two separate health incidents) and inside of one 12-month period; this after being very healthy and relatively injury-free for most of my life.

I started off the New Year in the emergency room through no fault of my own. Literally, on January 1st, I found myself admitted to the hospital and having unexpected gall bladder surgery the next day. Being that I am not one of the F's that doctors and nurses use to determine people at risk for gall bladder issues – forty, fat, female – this was a pretty unpredictable event. Breaking my foot later in the year during a soccer game was also unexpected. Both events knocked me off my feet for a bit and caused some feelings that I, as a pretty positive person, never thought I would feel. As I laid there in the hospital in January and wherever my gimpy-footed-self landed in October, I had the same questions run through my head – Is this ever going to end? Will I ever feel better? What is this going to look like on the other side? What are people going to think? What if this...what if that? I was out of my comfort zone. I hadn't been given the opportunity to predict that these things were going to happen, so I was not granted the benefit of foresight and preparation. If I had known what was going to happen, I probably would have eaten less fatty food and kicked the ball instead of someone else's foot. Seriously, I would have been able to avoid many of those self-defeating thoughts. I may have taken the time to read up on side effects of surgery and the probable recovery time. I may not have challenged quite so hard for the ball. I would hopefully have predicted and prepared.

When you start down a road you have not been down, or take a chance, or explore something new – you are taking a risk. You are challenged by your thoughts. You face the *default-to-negative* that we all seem to be hardwired with at times. I challenge you to use this section (utilize the **GET QUIET** areas) to truly try to predict what will happen when you act on your IT that you have identified. As you head into the land of doing versus hoping, doing versus wishing, doing versus waiting - there are unknowns. These unknowns are likely what have kept you from moving forward with IT in the past. You've probably talked yourself out of it because you didn't think you were ready, or you were afraid of what people might think or, even more likely, you had the fear of failure or success. This section will help you *flesh things out so you don't bail out.* Let's look at the would, could, should, probably will, might, might not – when you have a go at your IT.

Very seldom will the worst consequence be anywhere near as bad as a cloud of "undefined consequences." My father would tell me early on, when I was struggling and losing my shirt trying to get Parsons Technology going, "Well, Robert, if it doesn't work, they can't eat you."
— Bob Parsons

Chapter 2
They Can't Eat You

Throughout your life, how many times have you said, "What if?" to yourself, to your friends or to your significant other when you were making a decision to do *something*? I know I have said it a lot. For a long time, I was ridiculously concerned about what other people thought. Same with you? If not, you are one of the lucky ones!

What if
...I make a fool of myself?

What if
...I'm the only one who isn't trying it?

What if
...I dress up more than everyone else to impress the big boss?

A huge majority of the decisions that we make are driven by peer pressure. The microcosms of workplaces and neighborhoods are filled with unbelievable pressure. Identifying that this pressure continues to exist (even once you are in the working world and have a family) is a tremendous first step to getting out of its grip. Once you do, you will be wide-eyed to the other side – the fact that being different (by being the person who is stepping out and doing something you've always wanted to do) can be empowering.

I learned this first hand when I left a company early on in my career. It was the company that had the cool parties, hired the best looking people and had tickets to all the right games and concerts. I felt like I had arrived when I got that job. Very soon after, I realized that there were things going on inside the confines of that office that I did not need or want to be a part of. I found that on the other side of "What if?" is the "Hey, he's doing something different, that looks kinda cool" factor. Leaving that company seemed like a crazy thing to do to a lot of my friends, but I later found out that it was a coveted thing to do for many people whom I left behind. They wanted to get out, but couldn't bring themselves to do it.

I promise you that the people who don't say it out loud are thinking it – "Wow, she is finally taking the plunge and going to work for that non-profit. I wish I could do that." The neighbor who tries to talk you out of it is really just insecure with himself because he can't bring himself to do it – "You're really going to start your own business? Don't you know that 900% of businesses fail in the first two years?" The people who question you for taking a chance and going after IT will hopefully step up and be the first to congratulate you when you succeed. Heed the following warnings and you'll be amazed at how easy it can be to be your own person, large and in charge with this big thing you are getting ready to tackle:

WARNING:
PEER PRESSURE KNOWS NO AGE LIMITS

It happens in business! It happens at your neighborhood cookout! It happens on the golf course! You may feel peer pressure when you are 30, 40 and 50, not just when you're 20. It's different, but not really. There isn't a time that it ceases to exist. There is, however, a time that you can choose to ignore it. I assure you that as soon as you do, life is a blast! There is an unbelievable freedom that occurs when you stop worrying about what other people think or what they have or what they think you should have. I don't think you have to turn into a jerk and snub that 'thing' that other people do that you have elected not to do; I never did that after I quit drinking, for example. That's their choice. Your choice isn't necessarily the right thing, but it's the right thing for you. All that you can do is let your actions turn into successes that other people will take note of. If that leads them to being less materialistic, less critical, less pushy – sweet! If it doesn't, then it just isn't their time yet.

"Look carefully at the closest associations in your life, for that is the direction you are heading." – Kevin Eikenberry

WARNING:
PREVIOUS SUCCESS MAY HINDER FUTURE GAINS

Author Alan Deutschman said, "One of the reasons we resist change, unconsciously at least, is that it invalidates years of earlier behavior." Think about it, for years you have been the go-to gal at work. You always have the answers. You may have trained others inside of your company. You are extremely confident on the job. Your identity has been tied to what you do. When you put it out there to your friends that you are going to do _X_ they say,

You're going to do what?

*"But you're wasting all of those
years of doing _____."*

No you're not. Just because you have done something for umpteen years does not mean that is all you can (or should) do for the next umpteen years. The job does not make the woman – the woman makes the job. All of your experiences up to this moment have prepared you for the next moment – whether the work you have been doing and your next move are related or not.

There are two kinds of people in this world: those who want to get things done and those who don't want to make mistakes.
– John Maxwell

You can do IT without fear of reprisal, without worrying about peer pressure, without thinking that moving forward with IT negates the value of what you've been doing up to this point.

Tim Sanders says, "....break free from the shackles of short-term thinking" when he discusses The Law of the Long View in *Saving the World at Work*. As your mind has worked over the idea that you have a passion that you want to follow, it is likely that the initial mind-volleys back and forth have been about the ...

Emotional stuff – *What are people going to think?*

Unforeseen and foreseen pressures – *My spouse is going to tell me I'm crazy.*

Surface level questions – *What am I going to name it? What's my logo going to look like?*

It is when you can get past these initial (and totally natural) questions that you will get to the true meat of why you're getting ready to do what you're getting ready to do. You'll get to the impact on others, the reputation and legacy of what you are doing, the social value of it all. Tim says, "You don't want to be just well-intentioned. You want to make a difference. Only time can reveal the difference between the two." Since they can't eat you, go on and get started so that time can pass and reveal the merit of your IT and what IT is all about.

[GET QUIET]

So – what if? What are the *what ifs* that have run through your head as you have read up to this point? Take some time to work through the questions below. Be honest. Be silly. Ask someone else.

What will people think? (Go ahead, address the peer pressure thing straight away!)

What if my boss doesn't support me?

What happens if I leave my job?

What if I am hugely successful?

What if I fail?

What if I messed up and my IT isn't really my IT?

What if my significant other doesn't agree?

What's the worst that could happen?

Can they eat me?

The idea is to escape from your expertise and become a novice in an entirely different pursuit. It's about taking on challenges that you'll be bad at for quite a while rather than always returning to pursuits you've been good at for many years.

– Alan Deutschman

Chapter 3
What If.... You Don't Do It?

Your natural inclination is almost always to do what I just led you to do in the last exercise – think about the consequences of *doing*. It is hugely valuable to go through those motions – just ask anyone who has ended up in jail.

However, I did leave one question off the list in the exercise at the end of the last chapter – "What if I *don't* do it?" While I don't want to encourage analysis paralysis, I believe it is important to think about what happens if you stick with the always. The value of this kind of introspection is oft-overlooked in business and in our personal lives. We default to thinking only of the consequences of *taking action*, but we don't think about what happens *if we don't*.

In the book *Strengths Finder 2.0*, Tom Rath tells an interesting story,

> Mark Twain once described a man who died and met
> Saint Peter at the Pearly Gates. Knowing that Saint
> Peter was very wise, the man asked a question that he
> had wondered about throughout his life.

He said, "Saint Peter, I have been interested in military history for many years. Who was the greatest general of all time?"

Saint Peter quickly responded, "Oh that's a simple question. It's that man right over there."

"You must be mistaken," responded the man, now very perplexed. "I knew that man on earth, and he was just a common laborer."

"That's right my friend," assured Saint Peter. "He would have been the greatest general of all time, *if he had been a general*."

Why didn't he become a general? Was he insecure about exhibiting his leadership skills because of the company he kept? Did his talent as a laborer keep him from pursuing a career in the military? They say that luck is when preparation meets opportunity – he may have been prepared with his inborn talents but working with his head down when opportunity walked by.

We all have skills, strengths and talents that are just under the surface, but that we never tap into. We fear going from hero to zero. Seth Godin said, "The opportunity cost of investing your life in something that's not going to get better is just too high." Opportunity cost is a term taught in economics that describes what is risked if something does not happen – i.e. the opportunity cost of putting your money under the mattress is that you lose the ability to gain interest on it. What is the interest lost if you don't act on your IT? Who suffers from the lack of exposure to what you're good at – passionate about – put here for?

<u>You</u> do.

Your <u>friends and family</u> do.

Your <u>community</u> does.

The <u>world</u> does.

Not to cast doom and gloom, but let's look at the reality of that last statement:

You

$$Stress =$$

The effort you continue to put into tasks that are unrelated to your IT <u>minus</u> the pending reward of completing tasks that *are* associated with your IT

Stress from this, stress from that – so much of it is seems to come from stuff that we think is out of our control. This strain of stress is curable by replacing procrastination with doing. So when you think about just putting IT aside for a little while longer, take the time to think about how it will feel when you are actually working on IT or have completed IT. The warm-fuzzy feeling of doing something you love (and have been putting off) will make the stress you were feeling from procrastination seem like a distant memory.

Coach Jamey brought this all home for me when we had a conversation about how I was stressed out that I wasn't working on 'doIT'. He had me think about it this way – the longer you keep working on "something else," the longer it will take you to reach the point of reward that comes from doing what you really want to be doing. Strong stuff.

Friends and family

If we are indeed experiencing stress from spending time on everything *but* what we believe we should be doing, who bears the brunt? Hopefully you didn't say, "The dog." Yes, those who are closest to you – your friends and your family. If you don't take action on something that is burning inside of you, it is eventually going to boil over in ways that are not pleasant.

Community

Let's say you are a brilliant photographer but your equipment lies dormant in a closet for some reason. Your daughter starts attending a private school and there is a yearbook committee that you could volunteer for but don't.

The school is forced to pay for a photographer, thereby using financial resources that could have gone to buy books. More important than the dollars lost – the school doesn't get to benefit from your incredible talent. If you had stepped up, you would have had the chance to release that bottled-up desire and help others around you.

The World
Look it up. Almost every great accomplishment from the beginning of time has been a result of someone who reached the point where their IT became a compelling vision, and they acted on it. Whether that affected *their* world or *the* world was irrelevant to them.

[GET QUIET]

Who is the first person that comes to mind when I think about someone who should have acted on their IT, but didn't?

How do I feel when I think of that person?

Have I ever had an experience where I just blew it and, in hindsight, I know I didn't do 'that thing' because I was afraid of the consequence more than the potential gain?

Can I now step back and think about 'why'?

What is an example of a time when I did pull the trigger on something I had been putting off?

What is different now than at that time?

Why haven't I acted on my IT?

What wastes my time?

Exercise - Create a "don't do" list!

...you are more than what you have become. – Mufasa to Simba in the Lion King movie.

*Our deepest fear is not that we are inadequate. Our deepest
fear is that we are powerful beyond measure. It is our light,
not our darkness, that most frightens us. We ask ourselves,
"Who am I to be brilliant, gorgeous, talented and fabulous?"
Actually, who are you not to be? You are a child of God.
Your playing small doesn't serve the world. There's nothing
enlightened about shrinking so that other people won't feel
insecure around you. We were born to manifest the glory of
God that is within us...And as we let our own light shine,
we unconsciously give other people permission to do the
same. As we are liberated from our own fear, our presence
automatically liberates others.*

– Marianne Williamson

Chapter 4
SHINE

This quote is powerful in so many ways. Take a second and read it again.
Now let's break it down to see how it may help you overcome some of the
unknowns that you may *believe* you are up against as you venture toward
determining and executing your actions toward IT.

*Our deepest fear is not that we are inadequate. Our deepest fear is that we
are powerful beyond measure. It is our light, not our darkness, that most
frightens us.*

We live in a world of conformity and we have already identified that peer pressure abounds. Yet, in contrast, we constantly face "toppers." My good friend Gary Davis, author of the book *Networking in the South*, references the term "topper" in his talks. Gary defines a topper as someone who always believes he has done something that is better than what you did.

> You might be at a cocktail party telling an innocuous story about how you went scuba diving on your last vacation and the topper will inevitably step in and say, "Well my grandfather *invented* scuba diving."

> Your boss starts off his meeting by asking each person to share something positive that happened to them recently – you share how proud you are that you just ran your first 5k and the topper (your boss) decides it's a good idea to practically interrupt you and tell everyone in the meeting that he just did a triathlon.

> You are in a conversation with other Moms about your children – you share how much of a struggle you've been having at bedtime and the topper feels it necessary to share that they haven't had those problems in forever.

How is that helpful or valuable or necessary? It isn't, but many of us do it. Even if you aren't a topper, you may be guilty of thinking about the next thing you are going to say and thereby missing the last few words, or entire point, coming out of the other person's mouth.

So how is it that we suffer from this dualism, this contradiction of conforming-and-giving-into-peer-pressure versus the self-confidence-bordering-on-arrogance of topping others in conversation? Marianne Williamson is right – we aren't inadequate, we are confident and we try to show it all the time. However, when we are positioned to demonstrate our confidence through action versus just conversation, we begin to question ourselves. We shrink.

Your playing small doesn't serve the world. There's nothing enlightened about shrinking so that other people won't feel insecure around you.

From the stay-at-home mom who invented those decorative charms for Crocs and sold her company for millions in less than 2 years to pro football player Ricky Williams who went from college hero to pro zero; the examples abound of people who shine in the spotlight to others who are blinded by it. While the latter suffered from emotional issues that were later diagnosed, suffice it to say that once the stage was lit, he exited stage left.

When given the opportunity to do something that may bring success or attention, why might you halt plans to act on it? Are you afraid of being perceived as different? Are you concerned about what others may think?

Being conscious of the last part of Williamson's quote may just shine a light on why you should move forward with your IT -

And as we let our own light shine, we unconsciously give other people permission to do the same. As we are liberated from our own fear, our presence automatically liberates others.

You can create a movement by doing what you were put here for, by acting on your passion, by doing that project that you've been putting off. When others see you stepping out, doing something different from what you've been doing (or what others perceive as 'the norm') and then succeeding at the achievement of your Mt. Everest goals, they will want to do the same. While conformity has its place – albeit totally boring sometimes – differentiation and risk have their allure.

When I visited New Zealand during college, I had the opportunity to go bungee jumping. I had everything going for me in terms of being well-poised for risk-taking – I was 21 years old, male, in a foreign country, had my girlfriend with me and had gone sky-diving the day before – what a cocktail! The jump site consisted of a platform built over the edge of a cliff that led about 150 feet down to a river below. We were all jazzed up and watched about fifteen people jump successfully before us and then *SHE* got up there. *She* was an incredibly nervous twenty- something who was there with a bunch of her friends. *She* had the harness and cord hooked up and taken off by the instructors about three times - with a whole lot of screaming and crying in-between – before *she* finally took the plunge. Watching her go through all of those emotions and nervousness was pretty much the equivalent of putting a cigarette in the aforementioned risk cocktail.

I got over it and proceeded up to the platform right after *she* went and what did the instructors do? They said, "Hold on mate, it'll be just a minute while we change out the cord." I thought - *You're going to do what?!* I just finished watching Suzie Scared go through all those antics, then managed to get over my own trepidations that resulted and now you're going to change the cord that I just saw at least fifteen people jump successfully with? I thought, "Thanks a lot, mate" (sarcasm intended). Well, needless to say, I jumped and everything went well (save for the peep show that I gave everyone watching because I had those big, baggy nylon soccer shorts on).

My point? *She* showed courage and finally let herself <u>shine</u>. By doing so *she* liberated me from my fear which allowed me to jump. My jump then allowed others to go forth without fear and avoid the regret of not doing. This story, the stories of the little guy done good, the woman who went from homelessness to riches – they are all alluring and they lead us to a culture of doing.

To *predict* the future is a talent of few - to *worry about* the future is a fault of many. We all worry. We worry about the what- ifs. We worry about what others may think. We worry about negating the value of our previous years of work. While the fear of success is not likely a concern that comes to the top of mind when you think about taking action on your IT, it exists for many. **Fear *not*** because we can say the same for success as for failure, regardless of which you experience – "They can't eat you!"

[GET QUIET]

What do I think is going to happen?

What happens if I actually start working on your IT?

How will it feel?

How will it make others feel?

What good will come of it?

What bad could come of it?

Are there roadblocks that are immovable (or seemingly so)?

Based on my history, what do I think is going to happen?

Based on my new outlook from reading to this point, what do I think is going to happen?

Am I not going to do it because it's too hard or too far outside of my comfort zone?

To fear is one thing. To let fear grab you by the tail and swing you around is another. — Katherine Paterson

DO

Now that you know what *IT* is, you can figure out how you are going to *DO* it!

In a sea of mediocrity, just knowing what you want to do and then making an effort to pursue it distinguishes you from almost everybody else.

*–*John Maxwell

Determine

They won't make a change until they have hurt enough, heard enough, or had enough – all heart-level experiences. – Daniel Harkavy

Are you all in? Have you taken the time to identify this thing that you are going to do? Have you been able to predict some of the stumbling blocks that you might face? Now is the time to determine that you are actually going to DO IT.

A couple of years ago I took an online assessment called the 'Kolbe A Index' which identifies your personal mode of operation as well as your natural abilities. This was the first test like this that I had taken in my biz-life and it gave me a huge sense of relief when it essentially told me, "It's ok, Scott."

I mentioned in the introduction that I have always been an idea guy and that I wasn't afraid to put my ideas out there to my friends and family. My willingness (or *ability*, depending on how you look at it) to have multiple balls in the air at one time was perceived as a weakness by me and some people around me. The Kolbe assessment told me otherwise -

> *Your most effective efforts stem from your talent for juggling a flexible agenda. Rather than getting bogged down by having to put finishing touches on everything you start...*

That was all I needed to hear! For me, this was like the scene in *Good Will Hunting* where Robin Williams hugged Matt Damon and said repeatedly, "It's not your fault" until Matt was balling his eyes out. It's ok to have ten balls in the air and not finish absolutely everything I start? Yee hah!

For some, this kind of information may be a death knell to success (and it may give some Life Coaches an episode of the shakes), but it was a determination point for me. This weakness of mine was now a strength and it felt good.

I had hurt enough
from the frustration of being easily distracted by shiny objects.

I had heard enough
giggles and comments about all of my ideas and projects.

I had had enough
of the hoping, wishing, waiting.

I had now determined that I was going to do this thing; I was able to synthesize all of these thoughts and ideas into something workable and cohesive. Shortly thereafter, the aforementioned series of events transpired – my 1 o'clock in the morning Jerry McGuire moment, the development of the idea for *do IT groups*™, approaching Daniel and Todd, hiring Jamey, articulating my purpose & starting this book.

Do you want to know what was so refreshing about all of this coming together? I realized that it wasn't about money. I had determined that I was going to write a book, get on stage to share the message and start a bunch of *do IT groups*™ – all things that have pretty good income potential. Yet, the money became secondary. Previously, all of the ideas I had were all about the money:

Build a website and sell it to Google for a bazillion dollars.

Open a restaurant built specifically for business networking that could double as a comedy club and make a bunch of money.

Get the invention designed and patented and sell it to XYZ company for big bucks.

Call it a personal flaw or greed or whatever, but that was the way I had always thought about these things until I:

1) Realized that I kept coming back to the same thing, especially when I *got quiet*,
2) Had my *moment*,
3) Got help from others,
4) Tied these thoughts and ideas to something bigger,
5) Articulated my purpose and,
6) Quit worrying about this, that and the other thing.

You may just prove science right if you follow my lead on this:

A twenty-year study done by Robert J. Kriegel and Louis Patler that observed over 1,500 people to determine the relationship between passion, career choice and financial success.

At the outset of the study, the group was divided into Group A, 83 percent of the sample, who were embarking on a career for the prospects of making money now in order to do what they wanted later, and Group B, the other 17 percent of the sample, who had chosen their career path for the reverse reason, they were going to pursue what they wanted to do now and worry about the money later.

The data showed some startling revelations:

- At the end of the 20 years, 101 of the 1,500 had become millionaires.

- Of the millionaires, all but one – 100 out of 101 – were from Group B, the group that had chosen to pursue what they loved!

'nuff said.

[GET QUIET]

Notes:

Besides the almighty dollar, beware the following as you work toward taking action on your IT:

Complacency is the arch-enemy of completion

It is just easier not to. However, if you have locked on to the right thing – the thing you are really supposed to be taking action on – complacency will not even be a possibility.

Change most likely leads to success and fulfillment when WE initiate it versus having someone initiate it for us

Dr. Dean Ornish said, "People don't resist change, they resist being changed." Think about a time when someone suggested that you do something that you knew would improve your life –
"Come work for my company" or "Join my gym" or "Meet with my Financial Planner." Our friends, co-workers and family are usually well-intended when they say these things to us, yet we resist because it wasn't our idea. Barring the (very valid) God argument surrounding purpose, _you_ determined your IT. The changes required in your life to DO IT are self-initiated.

Analysis Paralysis abounds

There are a million reasons to wait. It's like deciding when to get married or have your first child – there is no perfect time. There is just the time that it is supposed to happen and it happens. This determination should be no different.

To wear three hats, you must have three heads.

Having three heads means you can have three headaches.

Chapter 5
'Fessing Up

Have you ever thought about how many job titles you really have? Oh, you might have *one* on your business card, but you probably have at least three others based on what is required of you each day.

During my many years of originating mortgage loans, I have gotten a lot of laughs from people upon asking them what their title or position is at work; they often tell me that they do *so many* things, they really don't know anymore. It occurred to me that my job was no different – it has at least 3 very distinct jobs inside of it – Outside Sales, Inside Sales & Transaction Coordinator. Many sales– related jobs are the same way. You have to be out in the field selling and marketing in order to maintain a flow of leads and referrals. Once the customer comes to you, you have to take the time to consult with them, do a needs-analysis and make a recommendation or "sell" the deal. Once they are committed to doing business with you, you have to manage that transaction through to a closing.

How many talents, skills and strengths are required in order to do all that is required, to wear those 3 hats? The answer is - A LOT! While you may do a fantastic job balancing all that is asked of you, you are among the minority if you are able to do all of it *well*.

So, when you begin executing on IT, you are going to need to go ahead and 'fess up on a few things:

1. You may have to let something go if you are going to proceed with IT

I am not under the delusion that everyone who reads this book is going to be able to just quit their job and dive head first into IT. Either way, if you are going to give IT the fair shake and effort IT deserves, something has got to give. Can you eliminate some routine tasks that are actually time wasters? Can you delegate things that are time-consuming or able to be handled by someone else? Can you use technology to automate some of your responsibilities?

2. Objects in mirror may be closer than they appear

I stated above that you may need to make some changes, including a possible move out of your current job or role, but I also believe that you may not *have* to leave what you are doing right now in order to work on IT. Tom Rath says, "You **cannot** be anything you want to be – but you **can** be a lot more of who you already are." Who knows if this thing that you've identified may be right under your nose in what you are doing right now? You may already be working in the field you need to be in to serve your purpose or to utilize your passion or to do the project that you are called to do. **Beware the obvious!**

3. You may be "just missing"

When I went through my first round of coaching, I was certain that I wanted to become a Manager. I had worked in my industry for almost 10 years and I wanted an opportunity to share my knowledge with other loan officers and help them grow their businesses. I proceeded to make a couple of company changes in order to get into management, got there and realized it was not where my experience, strengths and talents were best-served to help others – I needed to be in a coaching role. I needed to be facilitating or in some sort of coaching position and that is, ultimately, where I have landed.

Please be aware of this with your current role and where you are headed. There is a serious level of discernment, reflection and consideration needed when determining that you are going to move forward and act on your IT.

You may think your project should be to create your own company ....but maybe you just need to partner with another.

You may believe that your passion is taking pictures ....but maybe it is really in the creativity associated with editing them.

You may be certain that your purpose is to become a Pastor ....but maybe it is actually to be an author of religious books.

[GET QUIET]

What are my three hats?

Which one or two could I hand over to someone else?

What daily / weekly / monthly tasks or habits can I just eliminate and life would still go on? (reading the newspaper, taking long lunches, watching train wreck TV shows)

How could I better use technology to be more efficient?

What is it that I have always done (that's kind of bugged me) that I could just quit doing?

Can I tie my IT into what I already do at work?

How can I tie my IT into what I already do at work?

"Would you tell me please, which way ought I to go from here?" she asks.

"That depends a great deal on where you want to get," the cat replies with a grin.

"I don't much care where," she answers.

"Then it doesn't matter which way you go," the cat responds.

– Alice's encounter with the
Cheshire Cat from Lewis Carroll's
Through the Looking Glass

Chapter 6
Great Expectations

Have you ever really taken the time to think about how much you do without *really* thinking about the end result? Put another way, we often focus on what we *think* the outcome is going to be, but we don't really make it all the way to the finish line.

To help people with goal-setting, one of the most prolific examples used by authors, speakers and trainers is sports. Why is this? Because there is a clearly-defined finish line in most sports. Athletes are able to plug that finish line into their brain, body, training and preparation, thus allowing them to get precision focus from knowing where that finish line is. However, is the finish line what we think it is?

Football Player –
We think his finish line is to win the Super Bowl.
He thinks he has to focus on winning the battle at his position to ultimately be rewarded with a big contract for being the best at his position - the big contract is his finish line.

Golfer –
We think her finish line is to win the tournament.
She thinks that maintaining good course management and forgetting about bad shots, bad breaks and bad holes as soon as possible will put her in a position to win – winning the small battles is her finish line.

Hockey Player –
We think his finish line is to raise the Cup at the end of the season.
He thinks that putting in good shift after good shift and winning the battles in the corners will build momentum that will help the team – playing a fundamentally sound game is his finish line.

What word did you see in every example? Battle. No athlete is trying to, or can, win the whole stinkin' thing right out of the gate. It's not possible. It's not all under their control. They realize that they have to win the individual battles to win the war. Does this change your perspective a bit when you think about moving forward with your IT? If you concentrate on the small projects that lead the way to fulfillment and completion of IT, you'll have a much greater likelihood of success. You'll also have many more successes to celebrate!

A memory comes to mind from when I saw Tony Robbins speak in person (fyi – seeing him speak is like a Grateful Dead show – you need to do it at least once). We were seated in rows with people in front of us and behind us. He had us sit with our backs against the seatback and asked us to reach our arms out as far as they could go and then put them down. He proceeded to give a talk about how we *really* don't reach as far as we can and the value of having better expectations about our abilities. What do you think happened the next time we reached our arms out in front of us? We all touched the backs of the people in front of us. It's the same thing with creating expectations for yourself when you take the plunge toward your purpose, passion or project. You have to take the time to think beyond what you *think* the finish line is and get to the true outcome that you are seeking. The results will be beyond your *expectations*.

We don't know we have expectations until we're disappointed.
– *Jane Smith*

We often hear about the value of having a vision. I had no experience with creating one until I started being coached. One of the first things I had to do was to actually write out my vision for my business. It wasn't just – "I want to be a Manager one day."
It was,

> I have a production team of 3 people including myself that is producing $50M per year. All members of the team are cross-trained so that one person can be out and it does not affect the workflow or efficiencies of the team. I am involved primarily in a management capacity over the team and in meeting with business partners. I have a high trust call with the Client in the beginning of the process and the team takes it from there. Every Client leaves us as a raving fan and refers a minimum of 3 people from their sphere annually.

> My branch consists of 15 RM's, 7 processors, a producing sales manager, operations manager, administrative assistant and an office sales and marketing assistant. Five of the RM's have teams consisting of at least a personal sales assistant. Seven of the RM's are being coached and all managers are coached.

The bi-weekly sales meetings are run by the sales manager and are very proactive, involving sharing of best practices and regular product and sales training. Guest speakers are brought in bi-annually to motivate and train RM's. There is a great sense of team in the office because sales staff and operations staff meet together monthly....

... you get the idea.

Articulating these expectations, *IN WRITING*, turned out to be an incredibly valuable exercise when I experienced serendipity. As I mentioned earlier, I made a company change after about 10 years in my industry. My decision was based on much greater promise of moving into management at the new digs. I was prepared for this new opportunity and had the "Put me in, coach" attitude because I had gone through the exercise of creating my vision. Then the Manager, whom I was hoping to replace upon her move out of town, decided to stick around. During that same deflating week, I got a call from another company and ended up with an offer to manage a branch office for them.

What did I do? I pulled out the vision document, analyzed it against the new opportunity and took the offer. Because I had taken the time to get past the "I want to be a Manager" finish line and detailed my expectations for what I wanted my management experience to look like, the decision was easy. Your envisioned future acts as a tour guide for you in your decision-making.

[GET QUIET]

Notes:

My attitude was going South on a greased pole.

– John Eldredge

Chapter 7
Always Positive

Attitude - In my eyes, this is the easy part. Attitude is one of the easiest things to control and will be one of the most important factors on your successful journey to completion. I talked earlier about how we seem to be hard-wired to default to the negative view of things. Why is this? I don't know – we could pontificate that it goes back to Adam and the apple. In the meantime, I want you to determine that you are going to default to positive as you work toward your IT.

I have a memory from my high school years of a guy named Tom Haney. Tom owned one of the most popular health clubs in my hometown. He was a big guy with a deep, booming voice. His hair was Jimmy Johnson-perfect, he always dressed well, he had a swagger about him - and he drove me crazy. Why? Because he was always so darn positive! Whenever you would walk past him, he would always be the first to say, "Hey, how you doin' today?" Since the go-to answer in our society seems to be, "Good, how are you?" - he would always say *GREAT!!!* To most people this may have gone unnoticed, but I was fighting the hormone fight at the time and was in the doldrums of teen angst - my reaction was about the same to him as it was when Mom told us we were having pot roast for dinner.

After I worked through the aforementioned "issues" that I faced in high school and got to college, I had a turning point in my attitude - I met the guy who ended up being the best man in my wedding. I don't think I've ever called him *Steve* so I certainly won't start here – Pelle (short for Pellegrino) is the most positive person I have ever met. Over my four years in college, and especially in our senior year when we lived together, I realized the value in being positive – it's infectious, it's a lot more attractive than being negative and it leads to more opportunities and good fortune than negativity ever will.

In the last few years, and especially very recently, I have had numerous people comment about my positive attitude. That is testimony to my exposure to people like Tom Haney, Pelle and author and speaker, Tim Sanders. I had a moment not long ago when someone asked me how I was doing and I answered with a Tom Haney-like

GREAT!!! Life is good!

The guy's response was a barely-audible *ha* or *hmm* that seemed to say, "That's pretty much the answer I'd expect from Scott, I kind of like that." I *didn't* take it as though he was thinking, "Yuck, we're having pot roast tonight." Whether I was right or wrong, I don't really care because I'd rather have someone show disdain for me saying "Great!" than having them commiserate with me for the first 5 minutes of the conversation when, "Good, how are you?" is followed by, "I can't wait for the day to end, I'm really busy, the phone won't stop ringing, it's cold out........"

If you suffer from the negativity virus, keep these things in mind as you move forward and DO IT:

1. *Consider this your divorce from how it used to be*

If this thing you are getting ready to work on is really IT, it's important enough to cause some changes in your life. How you act and react, where you spend your time, who you surround yourself with – all are fair game for change. What you are getting ready to do is probably (hopefully) going to cause positive changes in other people's lives and that in itself should help you to realize that what you're doing is good and merits a positive attitude. Let's get into the "I can do it" mindset and out of the "ho hum, woe-is-me, I can't make this happen" mindset.

If you know, yet do not do, you do not know. — Oie Osterkamp

Don Piper teaches this mind shift in *Heaven is Real* – he calls it the "new normal." After years of suffering through the ill-effects of a brutal car wreck, he began to tell his story. His journey is nothing short of remarkable – a trip to Heaven and back, followed by trips around the world to help people who are suffering. His perspective on learning to accept a new normal is summed up here,

> *Your new normal may not be what you think it will be or should be. You will likely end up at a different place than where you thought. In fact, it's almost a guarantee because none of us can perceive what the new normal will be.*

2. *If it's gonna be, it's up to me*

Take note – the instances will be rare when someone else is as passionate about your IT as you are. Unless whatever you are working on is an absolute lay-up to a fortune or is something that is just life-changing, it is likely that you are going to get a tepid response from people when you share what you are doing with IT. *That doesn't mean don't share it!* You will find your cheerleaders. Just understand that it is ultimately going to be up to you to continue your focus on how valuable this thing is and to let the feeling of completion drive you and your attitude about IT. It's like you're playing center midfielder in soccer – you can go play offense when the team needs you there and you can go play defense when you are needed in the back – it's up to you.

3. *Give it away*

Have you noticed how much free stuff is available on the web? Information, advice and video all abound at no cost. The mindset of so many website owners is to give as much away as possible. It gives a feeling of freedom and makes us less averse to paying for something of value if we've received tangible, free stuff in advance of being asked to buck up.

As you went through the processes of identifying and predicting that I described earlier, it is highly likely that you have proceeded to have some internal conflicts about what you are going to act on.

You may have identified that your next project was to make and market Grandma's chili recipe into a business, but decided to go to culinary school instead.

You may have identified your passion for real estate and had an idea for a way to revolutionize the industry, but decided that building your personal cache of properties would create more of a financial legacy for your family.

You may have identified that your purpose for being on this earth was to follow through on your years of research, but decided to become a professor because you are more passionate about teaching than building.

What to do with those nuggets, those ideas that had a lot of value but that you have decided not to act on? Much like a kid hoards his toys so none of the other kids can get them, our compulsion is to keep the recipe, the revolutionary idea or the research to ourselves. Ask yourself, though - if the idea had value and merit enough to garner your consideration in the first place, isn't it worth it to get it out into the atmosphere to see what happens with it? Give it away! If you're not going to do it, share it. Be abundant and share the idea with someone who might do it or, God forbid, do it better! Hand it over to someone who may have the time, talent and treasure to make it happen. Stay involved if you want to or if you feel like it needs you, but don't let it own you – it wasn't your IT, but it may be someone else's.

If you want good results, you need to perform good actions. If you want to perform good actions, you must have positive expectations. To have positive expectations, you have to first believe. – John Maxwell

[GET QUIET]

How has my attitude been about change over the years?

Where does that come from?

What does my new normal look like?

Who is in and who is out (of my life) going forward?

What have I been hung up on that I can now just let go?

Am I hanging on too tight to what *I think* is my IT?

Have I asked others if it's time to let go?

What can I give away?

Execute

This is hard!

– Will Ferrell playing
George W. Bush on
Saturday Night Live

When I started out in the working world, my father gave me a little piece of paper that I have always kept close – it said, "The only place that <u>s</u>uccess comes before <u>w</u>ork is in the dictionary." What you are getting ready to do will require work, but it will be fun. If you have given proper time and effort to the Identify section of this book (and the exercises in it) the execution of your IT will feel a lot more like fun than work. This book in your hands is a true testament to that.

You may be getting ready to tackle something you have never done before - that is exactly what I did with this book. I really did not know what I was doing, but I knew I was passionate about my message. Quite honestly, I said to myself, "I'm going to do this now" – and I did. However, from start to finish, I faced -

> 4 ear infections and two strains of the flu with our kids, my wife having a bad bout with the flu, a broken foot, serious eye surgery for my Dad, the lowest income and production levels in my career, the highest income and production levels in my career, a change of offices, a dead battery in my car, open heart surgery for my father-in-law, emergency abdominal surgery for that same father-in-law, did I mention the busiest time ever in my career?, being interrupted by my kids literally right as my fingers hit the keyboard, my favorite team in the NHL playoffs (didn't miss a game), the holidays, soccer games, exercising, incessant mind-drifts about a special little girl with a brain tumor......

The list goes on and on - *and everyone's does!* We all have these kinds of challenges. They are thrown at us daily and all of them pose as potential hindrances to our success with executing on our IT. However, this book is proof-positive that it can happen. I was abso-freakin-lutely determined to get this sucker done. Yes, I got delayed. Yes, I got distracted. Yes, I got frustrated. Yes, other things took priority. Yes, Jeanne got tired of me bailing on her in the evenings in favor of the computer. Yes, I lost some sleep. YES, I GOT THIS DONE AND AM *HELPING OTHERS ACHIEVE* BY DOING SO. The absolute key is making sure that you have truly Identified IT, Predicted IT & Determined IT - if you have, Executing IT will be possible – and a lot more fun!

Never quit something with great long-term potential just because you can't deal with the stress of the moment. The life challenges that are going to be thrown at you on your journey will come and go. So often, when bad things happen or curveballs are thrown at you, it seems like there is a black cloud of doom over you that is never going away. You can't see beyond the challenge of the moment. However, when you have this thing that you've identified as being so important to you - your IT - it's like the experience many airplane flights produce:

It's a rainy day at the time of takeoff. It's dark outside. It's gloomy. You get up into the clouds and they are dark and gloomy too. Then, all of the sudden, it's bright and sunny. You're above the clouds and it is a whole new experience.

This is no different. You have the bright, sunny sky to look forward to – DOing IT!

It is no mystery that the *doing* is usually a lot more difficult than the hoping, wishing or waiting for some change to happen – *especially* the waiting. It is so much easier to just hope that something will happen or change than it is to take action and *cause* the change. It is so easy to wish for a new thing to come about in your life. It is so easy to wait and do it later. My hope is that these last few chapters that you are getting ready to read will get those kinds of thoughts out of your head and help to get you jacked about diving in head first.

It's a cinch by the inch and hard by the yard.

– Sally McGhee

Chapter 8
Baby Steps

Would you agree that it is usually the little things that don't get done that lead to stress? Doing those little things (that seem unimportant) will lead to <u>m</u>omentum and success. Not doing the little things leads to <u>n</u>omentum and stress. Taking the time to actually detail and itemize the little things is where we fall off the wagon.

On a daily basis, you put things in your calendar and on your to-do list that you actually <u>*cannot*</u> do! I don't mean 'cannot' in the sense of not being capable, but simply that they cannot be done ...without something else happening first.

You cannot...
create marketing plan

You cannot...
write book

You cannot...
post to my blog

David Allen wrote the bible on a ridiculously simplistic way of thinking in his book, *Getting Things Done*. Then, Sally McGhee took the concept a step further in her Microsoft book entitled, *Take Back Your Life* with tips on how to fully implement the strategies laid out in *Getting Things*

Done. Both books are built on the concept that I believe is best laid out in this (paraphrased) example:

> You have company stay at your home.
> At the end of their stay they let you know that the light bulb in the cathedral ceiling in your guest bathroom is out.
> You go in and check it and are mortified at how dark it is in the bathroom without that bulb working.
> You put a sticky note on your computer monitor that says, "Change light bulb in bathroom."
> Life goes on and the yellow sticky note fades to black because it's been on your monitor for so long that you don't really even "see" it anymore.
> Your friends come back for their next visit and it hits you that you never changed that bulb.
> Out of embarrassment you run to the home improvement store to buy a light bulb and find yourself in front of a sea of light bulbs and have no idea which one you need to buy.
> Your perils continue until you realize that your sticky note that you stuck on your monitor should have said, "Call Wayne the next door neighbor to borrow his ladder."

She couldn't possibly 'Change light bulb in bathroom'. It had a number of dependencies to it. Her "Strategic Next Action" (SNA) was to call the next-door neighbor to get a ladder so that she could get up there and see what she actually needed at the store.

In my eyes, this line of thinking is absolutely brilliant, much-needed and, WOW - way simple! I have learned in my experiences with coaching and in my do IT group™ that time/priority management is the common denominator in terms of challenges that we face when we try to get things done. We all feel as though we have so much coming at us and from so many angles. Is it possible that we feel this way because we haven't stopped and taken the time to determine the next step? The big project has much more brain weight to it than the next task does.

Pretend you're looking at your to-do list and you see this:

To Do
Create presentation for Executive Committee meeting

as opposed to this:

To Do
Next Project:
Prepare for creation of presentation for Executive Committee meeting
     Next Actions:
- Email Ella to schedule a time to talk on Monday
- Write out list of questions to ask Ella during call
- Talk to Ella to get input about her last presentation to the committee

The next key is to get those suckers into your calendar. You may argue the value of a to-do list, but there are two key components missed with so many to-do lists – a due date and the actual blocking of the time that you are going to use to handle that task. Sally McGhee says, "....there's a 75 percent greater chance of a task being completed if it's scheduled on your calendar rather than tracked on your task list or in your head." I wholeheartedly agree with that and also believe that you must address "By when?" and "When to do?"

If you commit to your boss that you'll have the presentation complete by March 15th, you'll be doomed if you don't put the reminder in your system to have it done by that date. You'll be double-doomed if you don't block the time in your calendar to actually complete the tasks needed to get the presentation done. Again, you're following the system of big thing – smaller thing – even smaller thing and so on - you're getting down to the granular level. By doing so, you are giving your brain a break and possibly getting some sleep at night because you have all of the detail in writing instead of in brain cells.

[GET QUIET]

What kinds of tasks do I put in my calendar that I can't really do?

Do I need to re-evaluate how I utilize my to-do list?

Do I make the distinction between due date and time blocking the time to actually complete tasks?

What resources could I utilize to help create better habits around getting things done?

*We often prefer to think that change is all about the
right process, but what's more important are the people.*

— Alan Deutschman

Chapter 9
Change Agents

Change. What feelings, emotions or bodily secretions does that word evoke for you? I look at that word and say, "I ain't scairt." I am a firm believer that change is good and that normalcy, complacency and sameness are boring. So much of what you have read in this book is really about change. You've been challenged and tasked with the idea of doing something that you have not been doing - that *is* change. What gives you the greatest likelihood of success with making a change? Other people.

Think about a success that you or someone close to you has had with making a change. Losing weight. Quitting smoking. Changing careers. These things are not often accomplished alone. Get around people who have similar challenges and interests and you will thrive. Alan Deutschman proved it when he studied inmates, factory workers and heart patients in the book, *Change or Die*. One of his big ah-hahs was that many of the people who were suffering in bad environments had never known anything different.

Many of the inmates were brought up in crime-ridden areas and never knew that there was any other way.

The factory workers knew nothing but negativity and angst because their managers had always managed by fear.

The heart patients hadn't yet experienced any negative consequences of their eating habits and sedentary lifestyle.

Once these groups were given education as to how it *could be* and more importantly, were grouped with other people like them who knew how it *could be,* they thrived.

When you are trying to move forward with your IT, you absolutely have to have people around you who will support you, hold you accountable and help you keep your eye on the ball. If you have shared your purpose, passion or project with the right people, they are likely going to become your cheerleaders. The people who believe in you are going to be the ones to help you to notice the ever-so-important *little things* – either the positive gains that you are making toward your IT or the missteps that may be working against your success – and help you to either celebrate or abolish them.

I want you to be open to the idea that these *may not be* the people who are closest to you. There are three reasons why these people may not be your family or even your closest friends:

1. Because they see you every day. Remember the saying, "It's a cinch by the inch and hard by the yard?" The slight changes are not quite as noticeable to someone who sees you daily as they are to someone who sees you every two weeks.

2. They may have seen you fail before. For example, if you have tried in the past to lose weight and get into shape, those closest to you have the curse of knowledge – they have experienced your failure and quite honestly, allowed it to happen. It may not have been purposeful, but

you gained all that weight back on their watch. This may hurt *their* confidence in trying to help *you* again or *your* confidence in them being able to help *you*.

3. You may not hear them. They may talk, but it may be like white noise to you because you are around them so much and you are so used to their perspective - the teachers' voice from the Peanuts® cartoon comes to mind.

[GET QUIET]

Notes:

＊

So you've decided to do IT – you're going to write that book. It all started when you were five and you used your little notebook and a pencil to write out page after page describing your first days in kindergarten – you drew a cover for it and everything. From there you wrote great papers through school and especially in college. You've always been good at writing letters. You've been told that you were a great writer. Recently, the frustration of having all kinds of recurring thoughts and ideas swimming around in your head came to a crescendo and you decided to synthesize all of that into a book. Oh wait, that's *my* story!

I cannot tell you how daunting of a task it felt like when I first thought about writing this book. I went through all of the emotions, processes and suggestions that you have read about so far. I will tell you that the absolute, most important ingredient to my success in getting it done was involving others. From day one I let my family, friends, neighbors, customers, business partners, other authors and speakers, even fellow Facebook-ers know that I was going to do this thing – and they latched on because I was passionate about what I was doing. That passion led to their buy-in and they became my cheerleaders. Because of this, I had people in every walk of my life saying to me,

"How's the book coming along?"

"Don't forget to send me a copy of your book when you're done."

"You done with the book yet?"

"Daddy, aren't you going to work on your book tonight?"

How could I <u>NOT</u> finish the book???!!!

These people are my change agents. I have gone from a guy with a vision to a guy with a bigger vision who is now an author and a speaker – that's a change.

These people are my accountability partners. It would have taken me twice as long to get this book done had it not been for their accountability comments, questions and prods.

These people are my people. I have bonded with them (some of whom I've never met) because I shared something I am passionate about and showed them my heart.

Over and over during the writing of this book and starting my groups I have identified that you really have to seize accountability opportunities when they present themselves:

When you make an appointment to go out on a sales call with your boss (because increasing your sales by 15% this year is your project you've identified) and your boss bails out on you at the last second...go anyway. You know she'll ask you about it next time you see each other.

When you are telling your co-worker about the play that you have just written (because you've always had a passion for the arts and writing and are finally acting on it) and they tell you that their uncle is a Tony Award-winning producer on Broadway...have them pick up the phone and call him on the spot. You'll now be forced to put some polish on it, ship it off and see what happens.

When you have your Jerry McGuire moment while sitting in church and decide that you want to finally pursue Divinity school (because you have believed for years that it was your purpose to have your own ministry one day)...mention it to your Pastor on the way out. You can count on him asking you how school is going every Sunday thereafter.

These kinds of moments present themselves all the time. Learning to identify them and then utilizing them for all they are worth is going to be a tremendous stepping stone toward your success with IT.

You've chosen to take action on your Purpose, Passion, Project. This is a HUGE step – congratulations! Now share it with others. They can, will and want to help you.

Read more about how others can help you in the Appendix –
"The Power of Groups – Introducing "*do IT group*s™"

If everything is under control you're going too slow.

– Mario Andretti

Chapter 10
The Law of the Squirrel

Pretend you're a squirrel - big furry tail, little whiskers - the whole deal. Your IT during the fall season is building a nest and filling it up with nuts to help get you through winter. You spend all your time finding the right tree to put your nest in, gathering the materials to build it and battling your brethren for the best nuts in the neighborhood.

One day you find the nut of all nuts – this one could get you through winter all on its own. You've built the biggest nest in the best tree. You are so excited. You grab that nut in your mouth and head across the street to get to your nest, get ¾ of the way across and remember that *other* nut you saw right before you found this one. You ask yourself, "Was that one bigger? Am I sure that this is *THE ONE*? Could I fit one more in my mouth and save a trip?" You do a u-turn and head back across the street and what happens? You get squashed.

It is scientifically proven that more squirrels get run over when they change their mind and dart back the other way instead of just continuing all the way across the street. Don't second guess your decision to move forward with your IT and end up flat as a pancake.

You've gone through the processes of identifying what this thing really is.

You've asked yourself and others some tough questions.

You've predicted what will and won't happen if you do IT.

You've predicted what will and won't happen if you *don't* do IT.

You've agreed that it is ok to shine.

You've determined that there are some potential roadblocks to making this happen.

You've 'fessed up on some things that you needed to 'fess up on.

You've set some expectations for yourself and committed to a positive attitude.

You've gotten in the "next action" mindset.

You've involved those around you so that you have support and accountability.

Now don't question yourself. You've done that already by going through all of the processes I just listed above. You've done that by getting quiet. You've done that by putting IT out to others. If you get going with IT and realize that you've "just missed," it's ok - regroup, retool, go back through this book and work it out. But, don't let the start stop you and don't get squashed by being indecisive.

Yesterday is gone.
Tomorrow is later.
NOW rocks!
DO IT NOW!

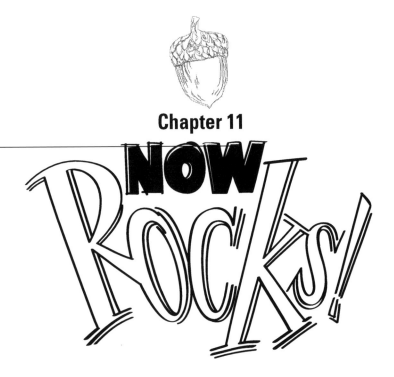

Chapter 11

NOW Rocks!

But, last time I tried to get going on this, my prototype didn't work just right and the company turned me down.

Ok, that was yesterday, you used the wrong kind of epoxy and the dude that turned you down is no longer at that company. That is a <u>yesterday</u> excuse.

But, I heard that Superball Pool Halls is planning on franchising soon and there will be one on every corner. They'll put me out of business in no time, so why should I even open my place?

Franchising can be an incredibly long, drawn out process that often convinces those with the most spectacular ideas to bail out and just keep it simple. That is a <u>tomorrow</u> excuse.

I have artistic talent that got me to the point of working side-by-side with Spielberg before I had kids. The kids are now in school full-time and I totally think that talent could come back out if I started writing and illustrating children's books.

You've used your talent in the past and it got you to high places. You've had life experiences since then that sparked new ideas. You have the time and opportunity to meld the two together. That is *so* <u>now</u>!

You couldn't have read to this point and thought that you wouldn't read, somewhere in here, *There's no time like the present!* There really isn't. If you wait until everything seems just right, you'll be 94 before you actually go ahead and try to become a rock star or a Priest or an author. You'll also feel like you are half-alive because there is this thing brewing in you that needs to come out - to be seen and experienced by you and those around you.

In the excerpt from my Jerry McGuire speech you read earlier, you learned that I tried to take my own life - twice. That alone would make a guy pretty in-tuned to seizing the moment and not putting stuff off. Add to that the experience of having eight people close to me die before I graduated college and you can understand that I really had some perspective on *not* waiting. As morbid as it is, I often think about what I was feeling at some of those funerals, especially the services for young people. I was sad, but I was also strangely energized - I got the "life is short" pang in my heart. When I have moments like this in life, I think about selling everything and moving to the islands to enjoy life without the noise. Just like productivity coaches try to instill the "day before vacation" mentality into your daily decision-making, the reality of letting this very moment - right now – go, without it being everything it could be, is a shaker.

There is nothing you can do about the past – it's gone, done, over. Put a fork in it, it's cooked. You can think about it all you want. Maybe you'll learn some lessons from it, but you can't change it. Let it go. The future is ahead of you and, while it *is* bright, it isn't here yet. It is fun to think about and there is huge value in going through visioning exercises so that you know how today's activities tie into a bigger picture, but it's down the road.

Then there is now. This moment. What you are doing right this second. You own it. It's perfect and it's yours. Your IT is valuable, precious and needed. NOW is the time to tackle it. NOW ROCKS! DO IT NOW!

You make believe that everything is ok until your cryin'. You make believe that life is too long until you're dyin'. – Limp Bizkit

Closing

Tell 'em whatchya gonna tell 'em,

Tell 'em,

Tell'em whatchya told 'em.

– My wife

So there I was, on the home stretch with this book. I had the NOW Rocks! chapter done and it was time to write the conclusion. Three days left before my self-imposed deadline. While brushing my teeth after another night of believing I was too tired to write - and therefore not writing - I had an epiphany. I said to my wife, Jeanne,

> *I have a crazy idea – what if my book didn't have a conclusion? Do all books have to have a conclusion? You should read the last chapter, it has some finality to it and maybe it could just end with that. It would be kind of different from other books.*

Well, as wives sometimes do, she pretty much stomped me down and presented me with the quote (above), borrowed from Writing 101. I've told you what I was going to tell you, I've told you and now I need to tell you what I told you – Introduction - Body - Conclusion.

CHEATER! What a cheater I was trying to be. I had come this far with the delivery of my message to you and I actually looked for a way out of really finishing it. Was it because my deadline was coming up? Was it because the intensity and frequency of accountability comments from my cheerleaders were rising? Was it because I didn't want to let go of this project that was like a cozy security blanket that I've held so dear for so long? Yes - it was probably for all of those reasons and a million more. However, the finishing fanatic in me took over and now you have this book in your hands. *I want you to please consider this lesson that I learned as one of your most valuable takeaways from Holy IT!* – you need a conclusion to your book. You need to finish.

Tim Sanders nailed the philosophy of finishing in The Law of the Last Mile chapter of *Saving the World at Work*. He said,

> *Unlike the first few miles, in which the team is inspired and has yet to encounter obstacles, the last mile is fraught with difficult details. People run out of gas, they lose sight of their objective, they find that the last mile resembles Zeno's paradox—you keep getting closer to the finish line, but you never quite seem to make it.*

You have read about the countless obstacles that I faced with getting this book written – health issues, hockey games and a bad case of the busy's at work. The paradox I experienced during the writing of this book surrounds the fact that, even though this book serves and fulfills upon my purpose, passion *and* project, the amount of gas in the tank *still* saw huge fluctuations over the eight months or so that it took me to get this sucker done.

You will face this, I promise. You will, and should, also be incredibly inspired to do what you are getting ready to do. It is what you were put here for, what you are passionate about and it needs to happen for all of the reasons that you have read about and identified. But beware the finish – it is hard.

You may want to go ahead and identify now that you may need help with the finishing. Tom Peters talks about having a *Mr./Ms. Last Two-Percent to ensure completion.* This may be someone whom you identify as being a good finisher, someone who is bought into what you are doing and willing to help you take the final steps. Or, *you* may be able to be the finishing fanatic along with the help and accountability you get from your fellow *do IT group*™ members. One way or the other, it is absolutely huge for you to identify *now* that finishing may be a lot harder than starting.

"The most common trait I have found in all successful people is that they have conquered the temptation to give up." – Peter Lowe

A Brazilian marathon runner can teach us a lot about the value of identifying, predicting, determining, executing and, most importantly, finishing. Vanderlei de Lima was on his 22nd mile of the marathon at the Greek Olympic Games of 2004 when he was attacked. He had been leading the race to that point, but in a freak occurrence, was tackled into a crowd of bystanders by an Irish Priest. Remarkably, he started running again almost immediately after being released from the attacker's grip. While he was not hurt, his muscles started to tighten and two runners passed him. Some would say he settled for the bronze medal, but he celebrated as though he had won the gold – the gold that he had locked up before the attack. He also received an honorary Olympic medal for sportsmanship.

Identify – he identified that there was something strange happening when he saw this man coming at him.

Predict – even though he had never experienced anything like this before, he had to attempt to predict what was going to happen.

Determine – once he was released, he determined that he was going to fight through and finish the race no matter what. He was going to treat this challenge not as a negative, woe-is-me kind of thing, but as a motivator to complete the race.

Execute – he proceeded to finish strong and celebrate his win. In doing so he became a national hero in Brazil.

Finishing fanaticism – there was no way that he was *not* going to finish the race. He had trained his whole life for this moment. He had overcome countless obstacles to get to this point. He had envisioned crossing the finish line and being victorious.

Everybody has won and all must have prizes!

De Lima got his prize - what's yours?! Figure out how you are going to reward yourself for doing IT – both in the celebration of the small victories and the big ones - and have fun with IT!

Appendix A
The Power of Groups

Introducing...

If you see a turtle on top of a fence post, you know he had help getting there. —Alex Haley

You read about my Jerry McGuire moment earlier. The whole of that story is that my epiphany was centered on wanting to help other mortgage loan officers. I had a vision to somehow synthesize my knowledge of the industry *with* my purpose of helping others achieve *with* the success and systems of Building Champions *with* Todd Duncan's vast reach into the industry. Go big or go home – that was my mentality as soon as I had the idea. The initial plan that I approached Daniel and Todd with was to create a group coaching environment for loan officers. To my knowledge, there was no formal entity that provided this kind of industry-specific forum on a local level.

Again, these were guys that made my hands sweat and my voice shaky, but I was hell-bent on getting the idea in front of them. After hearing the idea, Todd said that it would directly address the issue of the "shrink wrap factor" – you go to a conference, buy the books, CD's and DVD's and then get home, get busy and don't do anything with what you purchased or learned. *do IT groups*™ could be the fulfillment partner for speakers and presenters the world over.

"We come; we learn; we leave. It is not enough." — *John Eldredge*

Daniel perked up when he heard the idea and said, not in so many words, that this was an idea that his coaching company had kicked around for years, but tabled it because their forte was in one-on-one work. However, in his infinite wisdom, Daniel turned this into a business opportunity for his company and suggested that I get back into coaching with them to work on developing the idea. During that one year process, the idea mutated into something very different from the original idea – what is now called *do IT groups*™.

As I went through the visioning process with my coach, I realized that one of the most important things to me was to impact as many lives as possible in a positive way. Solely serving mortgage people was not far-reaching enough. I formed my first *do IT group*™ to do a beta test and I also started writing this book. What have I learned about the power of groups?

-Making yourself vulnerable to others is a key to change and success.

-Humble pie tastes better when others around you are eating it, too.

-Helping helps you (more later).

-The group is collectively wiser than any individual.

-There are issues that you will share in this kind of a group setting that you wouldn't, or shouldn't, share with your boss.

-Just articulating your challenges gives you clarity.

-Accountability is delivered in many different ways.

-Some people need a coach, some need a group, most need both at some point. There is a need for structured groups like ours.

-The layman's perspective is *so* needed and valuable.

-Business is, to a great degree, business.

It's always nice to have your suspicions confirmed. After about six months of meeting with my beta group, questioning my initial beliefs about how the group would work, reworking my goals and tinkering with the way we were doing things, a member of my PBD (Personal Board of Directors - everyone should have one), presented me with the results of a study. In the study, the researchers were trying to identify the key success factors for completing a project. Here is how their results looked:

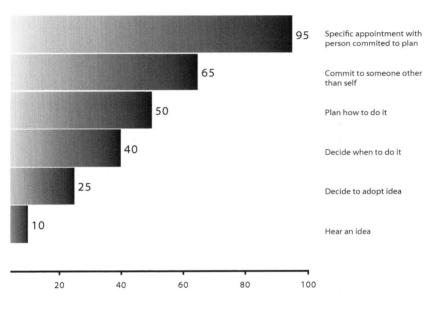

From the outset, my belief was that the involvement of others was going to be crucial to my own success and it was the crux of the entire idea for this book and for *do IT groups*™. This graph gave some serious credence to that notion – You have a 40% greater likelihood of success *when you share an idea with someone else* than you do by *just deciding to adopt an idea*!

Deciding you are going to lose weight
= a 25% chance of it happening.

Deciding you are going to lose weight
+ committing to someone else that you are going to do it =
a 65% chance of it happening!

We have found in our groups that these results are very accurate. We have also found that our group structure and agenda allow us to hit on all six of the success factors identified in that study.

write a book
take my invention to market
open my own business
get on the ladder to management
blog on a regular basis and monetize it
become a superstar in my industry
overcome my fear of public speaking
lose weight
come up with the next big thing
simplify life
run a half marathon

Please use *do IT groups*™ to get there. You will give and get feedback. You will be challenged. You will be held accountable. You will walk out of every meeting with a written plan for the next two weeks. You will be giving yourself and your IT the greatest likelihood of success that you can. Our mantra is "Helping Helps You" – we have repeatedly proven that the exercise of listening and then offering guidance to help others in your group is as valuable to the helper as it is to the helpee.

See for yourself:

Visit

www.doITgroups.com

for more information on
forming a group or joining a group
already meeting in your area.

Appendix B
Who did It?

Kevie Penny - aka 'Hubba Bubba' - was a shy and introverted home builder who became a full-time, professional clown who entertains children throughout the Southeast. He had his moment in church when it was announced that they were starting a clown ministry...for kids.

He ended up as the only adult participating in the training classes that followed and told his teacher that he was going to support his family by clowning – a difficult task, but one that he has accomplished. Kevie believes that all of his vocations to date serve him well as a clown (photographer, builder, roadie for a band). The skills he built while in those roles are all useful "on the job."

Hubba Bubba gets plenty of perspective on how lucky he is to be doing something he loves - plenty of parents share with him how unhappy they are at work and how much they wish they could do something so fulfilling with their lives.

Missy McGowan Dulansey says it "hit her like a truck." She had been a high-level graphic designer working with the likes of the Royal Family and the United Nations and got fed up with the red tape. She proceeded to get her Masters degree in Education so that she could serve elementary students who have special needs. She told me, "People can spend a lifetime not knowing what it is like to get up every morning and go to work without it feeling like it is work. I think I am more than lucky to have had that passionate experience in more than one of my careers."

Allen Smith was a full-time Realtor. He now rides BMX bikes competitively, runs a bike racing track, drives a bike-drawn rickshaw downtown, revived an old DJ business he used to have...and meets people in every one of those facets of his life who he can sell houses to. He didn't have to tell me in an interview that he is happier and more-fulfilled now than he has ever been, I can just tell.

Lisa Rousseau had her moment when her brother died. She identified right when that happened that she needed to honor his life. His death at a young age was very much attributed to his addiction to painkillers. So, she left all the trappings of corporate America and went to work for a non-profit that supports homeless people and those who suffer from drug and alcohol addictions. Lisa says that she does not have a job or a career, she has a passion.

Oie Osterkamp had never written a book and wanted to write one for his son. *Being a Sharefish in a Selfish World* is now a guiding force in his life and he has created a non-profit to further its message. He has also been very purposeful in building his primary business so that it ties directly into what he is doing with *Sharefish*, thereby avoiding the internal (and sometimes external) conflicts that can arise when you are "doing two things."

Acknowledgements

This book is a compilation of so many parts of my life – interactions with people, listening to public speakers and obviously, reading. I say *obviously* because of all the quotes that you see in this book. I hesitated to use so many, but they are the lifeblood of my messages and are seminal to so many of the things that make me, well, me. My hope is that having the work of so many authors compiled in this book is helpful to you - I highly recommend the books, speeches and tools that they offer.

I can't name everyone (*Matt*) who has influenced, supported and buoyed me throughout this process, but suffice it to say that I want to sincerely thank all of my peeps.

Tim Sanders - you make me want to be a better man...and I think you have.

Jamey Nordby – you have found your calling as a coach. Thank you for helping me find God and identify my purpose.

Daniel Harkavy – you and I have shared few words, but you have no idea how much you have influenced me.

Dave Anderson – you're just a cool dude and are entirely too smart for your own good. Thank you for your continued belief in doIT.

John Maxwell - for writing all of your books, but especially *Talent*.

Jeff Marsocci & Gary Davis – thanks for the nudge.

Oie Osterkamp – I don't really have words – I'm just plain glad to know you and thankful you are in my life.

Kevie, Missy, Allen, Lisa, Oie – thank you for sharing.

My parents – kinda can't help but thank the 'rents.

My (beta) do IT group™ – _now_ do you get _IT_?! Thank you from the bottom of my heart for supporting me and believing in what I am doing. Special thanks to Designer Debra.

the2thfxr, my neighbors, friends, friends on Facebook and anyone who ever asked me about my book – you have served as my accountability partners and didn't even know it. Thank you.

Now let's go start a movement – a DOING movement!

my
IT
is

_____

_____

_____

for a printable copy of this page and all the questions
in the [get quiet] sections of this book, please visit

www.holyITbook.com

Resources

Authors
Andy Beal – www.andybeal.com
Gary Davis – www.garydavispresents.com
Alan Deutschman – www.alandeutschman.com
John Eldredge – www.ransomedheart.com
Seth Godin – www.sethgodin.com
Daniel Harkavy – www.buildingchampions.com
John Maxwell – www.johnmaxwell.com
Sally McGhee – www.mcgheeproductivity.com
Oie Osterkamp – www.sharefish.org
Don Piper – www.donpiperministries.com
Tim Sanders – www.sanderssays.com
Rick Warren – www.purposedrivenlife.com

Coaching
www.buildingchampions.com
www.precisionfocus.net

Movements
www.savingtheworld.net
www.alwayspositive.com
www.sharefish.org

Training
www.gettingthingsdone.com

Tools & Assessments
www.precisionfocus.net
www.kolbe.com
www.strengthsfinder.com

Other Cool Stuff
www.nowrocks.com

Notes

Introduction

The wording "Disparate facts into related uses" came from the assessment I completed at http://www.kolbe.com - Kolbe A Index, (Kathy Kolbe, 2004)

I learned about the 70/30 concept that Building Champions coaches strive for from two sources - through personal experience and in Daniel Harkavy's, *Becoming a Coaching Leader* (Nashville, TN: Thomas Nelson, Inc., 2007), 161

IT

Winston Churchill quoted by John Maxwell, *The 21 Irrefutable Laws of Leadership* (Nashville, TN: Thomas Nelson, Inc., 1998), 199

Identify

English playwright James Albery quoted by John Maxwell, *Talent is Never Enough* (Nashville, TN: Thomas Nelson, Inc., 2007), 56

Emile Chartier quoted by David Allen, *Getting Things Done* (New York: Penguin Group, 2001), 72

The 3 P's – Purpose, Passion or Project?

Elbert Hubbard quoted by Sally McGhee, *Take Back Your Life* (Redmond, WA: Microsoft Press, 2005), 123

The words "went another way" were added by the author and replaced the words "started going wrong" as originally written by John Eldredge, *Waking the Dead* (Nashville, TN: Thomas Nelson, Inc., 2003), 165

Definition of purpose came from http://www.merriam-webster.com

The sentence, "If it all feels a little 'wispy,' remind yourself that a little humility can take you a long way" was paraphrased from the first paragraph on page 23 of *Waking the Dead* - John Eldredge, *Waking the Dead* (Nashville, TN: Thomas Nelson, Inc., 2003)

The book title, rather than the author, was credited because two authors wrote *You, Inc.* and it was not clear which one wrote, "Do what you love, and the pleasure of doing what you love will follow." Harry Beckwith, Christine Clifford Beckwith, *You, Inc.* (New York: Warner Business Books, 2007), 179

Definition of <u>passion</u> came from http://www.merriam-webster.com

All references to the movie *Jerry McGuire* came from *Jerry McGuire*, DVD, directed by Cameron Crowe (1996; Sony Pictures, 1997)

Socrates quoted by John Maxwell, *Talent is Never Enough* (Nashville, TN: Thomas Nelson, Inc., 2007), 59

Definition of <u>project</u> came from http://www.merriam-webster.com

Elmer G Letterman quoted by John Maxwell, *Talent is Never Enough* (Nashville, TN: Thomas Nelson, Inc., 2007), 123

The reference and analogy to "Driving your own car" came from Daniel Harkavy, *Becoming a Coaching Leader* (Nashville, TN: Thomas Nelson, Inc., 2007), 118

John Eldredge, Waking the Dead (Nashville, TN: Thomas Nelson, Inc., 2003), 69

Predict

Chinese Proverb quoted by John Maxwell, *Talent is Never Enough* (Nashville, TN: Thomas Nelson, Inc., 2007), 57

They Can't Eat You

Bob Parsons' "They Can't Eat You" rule is included with the permission of Bob Parsons (http://www.bobparsons.com) and is Copyright © 2004-2006 by Bob Parsons. All rights reserved.

Kevin Eikenberry quoted by John Maxwell, *Talent is Never Enough* (Nashville, TN: Thomas Nelson, Inc., 2007), 245

What If....You Don't Do It?

The Mark Twain story about Saint Peter at the Pearly Gates came from Tom Rath, *Strengths Finder 2.0* (New York: Gallup Press, 2007), 29

Mufasa to Simba in the Lion King movie quoted by John Eldredge, *Waking the Dead* (Nashville, TN: Thomas Nelson, Inc., 2003), 81

SHINE

The "...deepest fear" quote from Marianne Williamson is often mistakenly credited to Nelson Mandela. It was verified at http://www.nelsonmandela.org that this is indeed true and that Mr. Mandela did not actually utter these words. The source of this quote for use in this book (credited to Mr. Mandela) came from John Eldredge, *Waking the Dead* (Nashville, TN: Thomas Nelson, Inc., 2003), 87

Katherine Paterson quoted by John Maxwell, *Talent is Never Enough* (Nashville, TN: Thomas Nelson, Inc., 2007), 51

Determine

The findings about, "Your most effective efforts stem from..." came from the assessment I completed at http://www.kolbe.com - Kolbe A Index, (Kathy Kolbe, 2004)

"It's not your fault" was spoken repeatedly by Robin Williams in a scene with Matt Damon in *Good Will Hunting*, DVD, directed by Gus Van Sant (1997; Miramax, 1998)

The "Twenty-year study" was done by Robert J. Kriegel and Louis Patler and the results were printed by John Maxwell, *Talent is Never Enough* (Nashville, TN: Thomas Nelson, Inc., 2007), 35

Dr. Dean Ornish quoted by Alan Deutschman, *Change or Die* (New York: HarperCollins, 2007), 94

Great Expectations

The story about the Cheshire Cat from Alice in Wonderland has appeared in many business books. In this instance, it was quoted by John Maxwell,

Talent is Never Enough (Nashville, TN: Thomas Nelson, Inc., 2007), 75

Jane Smith, Business Roundtable meeting, June 23, 2009.

Always Positive

Oie Osterkamp, coffee conversation, November 10, 2008

Execute

"This is hard!" was spoken by Will Ferrell when he impersonated President George W. Bush on numerous occasions on NBC's *Saturday Night Live* -http://www.nbc.com/saturday_night_live

Seth Godin, *The Dip* (New York: Penguin Group, 2007), 64

Baby Steps

The light bulb example is the best analogy I have come across to illustrate the next-action mindset. I paraphrased from Sally McGhee, *Take Back Your Life* (Redmond, WA: Microsoft Press, 2005), 132

'Strategic next action' references - Ibid, 132-133. This term was also used repeatedly by David Allen, *Getting Things Done* (New York: Penguin Group, 2001)

The Law of the Squirrel

Mario Andretti quoted by David Allen, *Ready for Anything* (New York: Simon & Schuster Audio, 2003)

Original quote read, "It's the start that often stops people." John Maxwell, *Talent is Never Enough* (Nashville, TN: Thomas Nelson, Inc., 2007), 63

NOW Rocks!

Limp Bizkit lyrics come from the song *Rearranged* - heard on the radio and found at http://www.lyricsmuse.com

Closing

"Mr./Ms. Last Two-Percent" example from Tom Peters quoted by Tim Sanders, *Saving the World at Work* (New York: Doubleday, 2008), 114

"Finishing fanaticism" - Ibid, 115

Peter Lowe quoted by John Maxwell, *Talent is Never Enough* (Nashville, TN: Thomas Nelson, Inc., 2007), 118

Brazilian marathon runner story – http://www.wikipedia.org

Alan Deutschman, *Change or Die* (New York: HarperCollins, 2007), 20

The Power of Groups

Alex Haley quoted by John Maxwell, *Talent is Never Enough* (Nashville, TN: Thomas Nelson, Inc., 2007), 119

The graph which illustrates the factors that increase the likelihood of success is referenced widely on the internet and originated with a study done in conjunction with the American Society for Training & Development - http://www.astd.org

Harry Beckwith, Christine Clifford Beckwith, *You, Inc.* (New York: Warner Business Books, 2007), 173

Books

David Allen, *Getting Things Done* (New York: Penguin Group, 2001)

Harry Beckwith, Christine Clifford Beckwith, *You, Inc.* (New York: Warner Business Books, 2007)

Gary Davis, *Networking in the South* (USA: Highnet Promotions, 2007)

Alan Deutschman, *Change or Die* (New York: HarperCollins, 2007)

John Eldredge, *Waking the Dead* (Nashville, TN: Thomas Nelson, Inc., 2003)

Seth Godin, *The Dip* (New York: Penguin Group, 2007)

Daniel Harkavy, *Becoming a Coaching Leader* (Nashville, TN: Thomas Nelson, Inc., 2007)

John Maxwell, *Talent is Never Enough* (Nashville, TN: Thomas Nelson, Inc., 2007)

John Maxwell, *The 21 Irrefutable Laws of Leadership* (Nashville, TN: Thomas Nelson, Inc., 1998)

Sally McGhee, *Take Back Your Life* (Redmond, WA: Microsoft Press, 2005)

Don Piper and Cecil Murphey, Heaven is Real (New York: Penguin, 2007)

Tom Rath, *Strengths Finder 2.0* (New York: Gallup Press, 2007)

Tim Sanders, *Saving the World at Work* (New York: Doubleday, 2008)

Websites

http://www.astd.org

http://www.bobparsons.com

http://www.kolbe.com

http://www.lyricsmuse.com

http://www.merriam-webster.com/

http://www.nbc.com/saturday_night_live

http://www.wikipedia.org/

Audiobook

David Allen, *Ready for Anything* (New York: Simon & Schuster Audio, 2003)

Movies

Ferris Bueller's Day Off, DVD, directed by John Hughes (1986; Paramount Pictures, 1999)

Good Will Hunting, DVD, directed by Gus Van Sant (1997; Miramax, 1998)

Jerry McGuire, DVD, directed by Cameron Crowe (1996; Sony Pictures, 1997)

Afterword

Suffice it to say that one of the greatest challenges authors face is coming up with a title. It needs to grab people's attention. It needs to be memorable. It needs to describe what the book is about. 'Holy IT' does all of those things and, frankly, was arrived upon just days before this book was sent to the printer.

The use of the word 'Holy' was mainly intended as an adjective much like "Holy Cow!" or "Holy Super-Sticky Book Title, Batman!" It was also intended to stress the importance and significance of 'IT' in your life. While the spin off of 'Holy IT' as a curse is part of what may make it memorable, it is unintentional and no irreverence to 'Holy' is intended.

My hope is that no one is offended by the title. I am a Christian. I curse very rarely. I do not use the Lord's name in vein. To be totally honest, I was laying in bed praying for God to put a title into my head and heart when 'Holy IT' came to me. Yes, I had a Jerry McGuire moment to start this journey and to end it. Thank you, God.

Holy IT!

The Amazing Power of ClarITy

FOR TEENS

A Guide to Finding and
Doing Your Thing – Your 'IT'

SCOTT WITTIG

Coming Soon!

You're still here?

It's over.

Go on.

Go.

– Ferris Bueller

Made in the USA
Charleston, SC
31 January 2010